SPIRITUAL WARFARE

by

Derek Prince

Whitaker House

Scripture quotations marked (NAS) are taken from the *New American Standard Bible*, © The Lockman Foundation, 1960, 1962, 1963, 1968, 1971, 1972, 1973, 1975, 1977, and used by permission.

Scripture quotations marked (NIV) are taken from the Holy Bible, *New International Version*, © International Bible Society, 1973, 1978, 1984 and used by permission.

Scripture quotations marked (TLB) are from *The Living Bible*, © Tyndale House Publishers, Wheaton, Illinois, 1971 and used by permission.

Scripture quotations marked (KJV) are taken from the *King James Version* of the Bible.

SPIRITUAL WARFARE

Derek Prince Ministries–International
P.O. Box 19501
Charlotte, NC 28219-9501

ISBN: 0-88368-256-7
Printed in the United States of America
Copyright © 1987 by Derek Prince Ministries–International

Whitaker House
580 Pittsburgh Street
Springdale, PA 15144

7 8 9 10 11 12 13 14 / 05 04 03 02 01 00 99 98 97 96

Contents

Part 1: THE NATURE OF THE WAR

Part 2: OUR DEFENSIVE ARMOR

Part 3: WEAPONS OF ATTACK

Part 1:

THE NATURE OF THE WAR

Chapter 1

Two Opposing Kingdoms

There are many pictures of God's people in the New Testament. In Ephesians, for instance, God's people are presented through the following pictures: a legislative assembly, a family, a temple, and as the bride of Christ. However, the final picture of God's people in Ephesians is that of an army.

This army is committed to fight a war that is global in its proportions, which affects and includes every portion of this globe on which we live. In fact, even the word "global" does not do justice to the scope of this conflict. It embraces not only the earth, but extends beyond the earth into the very heavens. In fact, the adjective which correctly describes this conflict is not "global" but "universal." It includes the entire created universe.

The Scripture which most clearly introduces this conflict and describes its nature is

Ephesians 6:10-12. I will cite first the New International Version, then I will compare some other versions.

> 10 Finally, be strong in the Lord and in his mighty power.
> 11 Put on the full armor of God so that you can take your stand against the devil's schemes. (NIV)

Paul takes it for granted that, as Christians, we are involved in a war for which we need the appropriate armor, and that our adversary is the devil himself. He then goes on in verse 12 to explain more fully the nature of this war:

> 12 For our struggle is not against flesh and blood, but against the rulers, against the authorities, against the powers of this dark world and against the spiritual forces of evil in the heavenly realms. (NIV)

In the New American Standard version, this verse reads:

> 12 For our struggle is not against flesh and blood, but against the rulers, against the powers, against the world forces of this darkness, against the spiritual forces of wickedness in the heavenly places. (NAS)

The Living Bible, which is not exactly a literal translation but a paraphrase, reads:

> 12 For we are not fighting against people made of flesh and blood, but against persons without bodies—the evil rulers of the unseen world, those mighty satanic beings and great evil princes of darkness who rule this world, and against huge numbers of wicked spirits in the spirit world. (TLB)

Whichever version you wish to follow, it is clear that as Christians we are engaged in a titanic conflict which staggers the mind to consider.

I have meditated so often and so long on Ephesians 6:12 in the original Greek that I have come up with my own paraphrase. You might call this "the Prince version."

> For our wrestling match is not against flesh and blood, not against persons with bodies, but against rulers with various areas and descending orders of authority, against the world-dominators of this present darkness, against spiritual forces of wickedness in the heavenlies.

Let me explain why I chose some of those words. I say, "rulers with various areas and descending orders of authority," because that pictures a very highly structured and well-organized kingdom with descending orders of authority and different rulers and sub-rulers

9

responsible for different areas of their territory. I used the word "dominators" in "the world dominators of this present darkness," because the term "dominate" so vividly describes the way Satan treats the human race.

Notice that all translations except the Living Bible emphasize that the headquarters of this highly-organized kingdom is in the heavenlies.

Here are some points that emerge from Ephesians 6:12. First, the conflict involves all Christians—not some special group like missionaries, pastors or evangelists—but all of us. Many Christians have not seen it that way.

The King James Version of verse 12 states, "For we wrestle not against flesh and blood. . . ." I once heard someone comment that most Christians punctuate that verse wrong. They read, "We wrestle not — period." In other words, all we need do is sit in the church pew and sing hymns. However, Paul says, "We're in a wrestling match but it's not against flesh and blood."

Consider also the import of the word "wrestling match." Wrestling is the most intense of all forms of conflict between two persons. Every part of the body, every skill, and every trick must be used for success. It is a total conflict.

Satan has a highly-organized kingdom. In that kingdom there are various areas and levels of authority. The headquarters of this kingdom are in the heavenly regions. That is a staggering fact, but it is quite clear.

The fact that Satan heads a highly-organized kingdom astonishes some people, yet there are many clear indications of this in the Scriptures. In Matthew 12:22-28, this incident in the ministry of Jesus is recorded. Jesus had brought healing to a demon-possessed man who was blind and mute by driving out the evil spirit.

> 23 All the people were astonished and said, "Could this be the Son of David?"
> 24 But when the Pharisees heard this, they said, "It is only by Beelzebub, the prince of demons, that this fellow drives out demons." (NIV)

Beelzebub means, literally, "lord of flies." It is the title of Satan particularly as the ruler over demons because the demons are compared to the whole insect domain. Jesus responds to the Pharisees in verse 25:

> 25 Jesus knew their thoughts and said to
> them, "Every kingdom divided against
> itself will be ruined, and every city or
> household divided against itself will not
> stand.
> 26 "If Satan drives out Satan, he is
> divided against himself. How then can his
> kingdom stand?" (NIV)

There is a clear implication that, first, Satan
has a kingdom. Second, it is not divided but
highly organized. Third, it stands and has not
yet been overthrown. Jesus continues:

> 27 "And if I drive out demons by
> Beelzebub, by whom do your people drive
> them out? So then, they will be your judges.
> 28 "But if I drive out demons by the
> Spirit of God, then the kingdom of God has
> come upon you." (NIV)

Jesus here mentions another kingdom, the
kingdom of God. In particular, He describes
one point where the conflict between these two
kingdoms is brought out into the open. He
says, "When I drive out demons by the Spirit
of God, then you know the kingdom of God has
come." The implication is that the ministry of
driving out demons brings the forces of Satan's
kingdom out into the open and also
demonstrates the superiority of the kingdom of
God because the demons are driven out under
the authority of the kingdom of God. In the

final analysis, there are two kingdoms in opposition: the kingdom of God and the kingdom of Satan.

Again, in Colossians 1:12-14, Paul says:

> 12 ... giving thanks to the Father, who has qualified you to share in the inheritance of the saints in the kingdom of light.
> 13 For he has rescued us from the dominion of darkness and brought us into the kingdom of the Son he loves,
> 14 in whom we have redemption, the forgiveness of sins.   (NIV)

Notice again, there are two domains or kingdoms. There is the kingdom of light, in which our inheritance lies, but there is also the dominion of darkness. The word translated "dominion" is the Greek word *exusia*, which means "authority." In other words, whether we like it or not, Satan has authority. He is the ruler of a kingdom which the Bible recognizes. So these two kingdoms are engaged in mortal warfare and the war is coming to its climax in our day as this age comes to a close.

Chapter 2

Satan's Headquarters

In Ephesians 6:12, Paul makes it very clear that, as Christians, we are involved in a life and death struggle with a highly-organized kingdom peopled by evil, rebellious spirit-beings and that the headquarters of this kingdom is in the heavenly realm.

The phrase, "the heavenly realm," raises a particular problem in the minds of Christians. If Satan was cast out of heaven long ago, how then can he still occupy a place in the heavenly realm?

Let me answer this question by pointing out some passages that describe events that took place long after the initial rebellion and casting down of Satan by God. These passages indicate that Satan still had access to the presence of God in heaven at that time. Job 1:6-7:

> 6 One day the angels came to present themselves before the Lord, and Satan also came with them.

> 7 The Lord said to Satan, "Where have you come from?" Satan answered the Lord, "From roaming through the earth and going back and forth in it." (NIV)

Almost exactly the same incident is recorded again in Job 2:1-2:

> 1 On another day the angels came to present themselves before the Lord, and Satan also came with them to present himself before him.
> 2 And the Lord said to Satan, "Where have you come from?" Satan answered the Lord, "From roaming through the earth and going back and forth in it."
> (NIV)

So at that time, which was in the days of Job, we see that Satan still had direct access to the presence of the Lord. When God's angels came to present themselves and report to the Lord, Satan was there among them. The passage seems to indicate that the other angels did not identify Satan. I can understand this because in 2 Corinthians 11:14, Paul says that Satan is transformed as "an angel of light." The passage creates in my mind the impression that the only one who could identify Satan was the Lord. Apparently, he could appear in the presence of God mingling with the other angels and not be detected.

The Lord said, "Where have you come from, Satan?" In other words, "What are you doing here?" The Lord did not immediately banish Satan from His presence, but actually had a conversation with him. Therefore, we know that in the time of Job, Satan still had access to the presence of God in heaven.

> 10 Then I heard a loud voice in heaven say: "Now have come the salvation and the power and the kingdom of our God, and the authority of his Christ. For the accuser of our brothers, who accuses them before our God day and night, has been hurled down." (Revelation 12:10 NIV)

The "accuser of our brothers" is Satan. Notice that at this time he is still accusing God's people before God day and night.

Revelation 12:11-12 continues:

> 11 "They overcame him [Satan] by the blood of the Lamb and by the word of their testimony; they did not love their lives so much as to shrink from death.
> 12 "Therefore rejoice, you heavens and you who dwell in them! But woe to the earth and the sea, because the devil has gone down to you! He is filled with fury, because he knows that his time is short." (NIV)

That passage indicates that Satan still has access to the presence of God, and he uses his access to accuse God's people in the presence of God. Clearly, all the above passages that I have quoted refer to periods long after the original rebellion of Satan. So what is the answer? There is more than one heaven. I believe this is clearly indicated all through Scripture. For instance, in the first verse of the Bible, Genesis 1:1, it says, "In the beginning God created the heavens and the earth." The Hebrew word for heavens is *shamayim.* "Im" is the plural ending. The first time heaven is introduced, it is introduced in the plural.

In 2 Chronicles 2:6, we have this utterance of Solomon in his prayer to the Lord at the dedication of the temple: "But who is able to build a temple for him [the Lord], since the heavens, even the highest heavens, cannot contain him?" (NIV)

Where the translation says, "the highest heavens," the Hebrew says, literally, "the heaven of heavens." Either translation clearly indicates there is more than one heaven. The word "heaven" of the phrase "heaven of heavens" suggests a heaven that is as high above heaven as heaven is above earth.

18

In 2 Corinthians 12:2-4, Paul is even more specific:

> 2 I know a man in Christ who fourteen years ago was caught up to the third heaven. Whether it was in the body or out of the body I do not know — God knows.
> 3 And I know that this man — whether in the body or apart from the body I do not know, but God knows —
> 4 was caught up to Paradise. He heard inexpressible things, things that a man is not permitted to tell.　　　　(NIV)

Before I became a preacher, I was a logician and sometimes I cannot get away from logic. Logic convinces me that if there is a third heaven, there must be a first and a second. So there are at least three heavens. Apparently, the third heaven is where Paradise, the place of rest of the departed righteous, is now located. It is also where God Himself dwells.

Ephesians 4:10 speaks about the death and resurrection of Jesus:

> 10 He who descended is the very one who ascended higher than all the heavens, in order to fill the whole universe.　　(NIV)

Notice that phrase "all the heavens." The word "all" can only be correctly used of at least three. When I was teaching English to

African students in Kenya, a student once said to me, "**All** my parents have come to see me." I said, "You can't say 'All my parents,' because no one has more than two parents. If you only have two you can't say 'All.'" The same applies to the phrase "all the heavens." There must be at least three. I think that is clearly indicated by the whole tenor of Scripture. That leads us to the answer of the problem of how Satan's kingdom is still in the heavenly realm.

In colloquial speech, we sometimes use the phrase "seventh heaven" to describe a condition of great happiness. I suggest that is not scriptural. Actually, that phrase is taken from the Koran, the sacred book of Islam, and is probably not appropriate for Christians. Instead, if you are feeling particularly happy, let me suggest that you say you are "on cloud nine." There are plenty of clouds in heaven and that expression is more in line with Scripture. Jesus is coming in the clouds.

That there are three heavens is my opinion and not an established doctrine. However, I believe it to be a reasonable opinion which fits all the known facts of Scripture and experience. What are the three heavens? The first heaven is the visible and natural heaven with the sun, the moon, and the stars which we see with our eyes.

The third heaven, we know from 2 Corinthians 12, is God's dwelling place. It is Paradise, the place of rest of the departed righteous. It is the place to which the man was caught up and heard God speaking words that could not be uttered.

So we are left with the second heaven. Clearly, this must be between the first and the third. I understand it to be an intermediate heaven between the heaven of God's dwelling and the visible heaven that we see here on earth. I also believe this intermediate heaven is where Satan's headquarters are located. This would explain why we often find ourselves in an intense wrestling match when we pray.

Sometimes we do not realize how hard it is to break through to God. Sometimes we pray a prayer that is in the will of God, we believe God hears, and yet the answer tarries. There can be more than one explanation for that, but one major reason for experiences of this kind in the life of sincere committed believers is that we are involved in a warfare and that the headquarters of Satan's kingdom is located between the visible heaven and the heaven of God's dwelling.

Chapter 3

Battle of Angels

The book of Daniel has a specific example of spiritual warfare that casts further light on the location of Satan's kingdom. In fact, it describes a battle of angels. In chapter 10, Daniel describes how he set himself to pray and seek God for a revelation concerning the future of His people Israel. For three weeks he devoted himself with special intensity to prayer and waiting on God. At the end of the three weeks an angel from heaven came to Daniel with the answer to his prayer. The angel was so glorious and powerful that all the people with Daniel were scattered and he was the only one who remained to receive the revelation. Daniel 10:2-6 states:

> 2 In those days I, Daniel, had been mourning for three entire weeks.
> 3 I did not eat any tasty food, nor did meat or wine enter my mouth, nor did I use any ointment at all, until the entire three weeks were completed.

> 4 And on the twenty-fourth day of the first
> month, while I was by the bank of the great
> river, that is, the Tigris,
> 5 I lifted my eyes and looked, and behold,
> there was a certain man dressed in linen,
> whose waist was girded with a belt of pure
> gold of Uphaz.
> 6 His body also was like beryl, his face had
> the appearance of lightning, his eyes were
> like flaming torches, his arms and feet like
> the gleam of polished bronze, and the sound
> of his words like the sound of a tumult.
>
> (NAS)

As I have already mentioned, Daniel's companions could not stand this glorious apparition and just disappeared. Then the angel began to speak to Daniel and the part on which I want to focus is verses 12-13:

> 12 Then he said to me, "Do not be afraid,
> Daniel, for from the first day that you set
> your heart on understanding this and on
> humbling yourself before your God, your
> words were heard, and I have come in
> response to your words."   (NAS)

It is important to see that the first day that Daniel started praying, his prayer was heard and the angel was dispatched with the answer. However, the angel did not arrive on earth with Daniel "for three entire weeks," or twenty-one days. What kept the angel three weeks on the journey? He was opposed by

24

Satan's angels. Somewhere in the journey from the heaven of God to earth, the angel was required to go through Satan's kingdom in the heavenlies. There he was opposed by evil angels who tried to prevent him from getting through with a message to Daniel. Verse 13 continues:

> 13 "But the prince of the kingdom of Persia was withstanding me for twenty-one days; [The angel took twenty-one days because he had resistance and opposition in the heavenlies.] then behold, Michael, one of the chief princes [or archangels], came to help me, for I had been left there with the kings of Persia." (NAS)

All this took place in the heavenly realms. The leader of Satan's angels is called "the prince of the kingdom of Persia," the chief ruler over Persia. Related to him and apparently under him, were various "kings" or lesser angels. Then, on God's side, the angel that came to help the original angel was the archangel Michael.

In Daniel 12:1, we read this about Michael:

> 1 "Now at that time Michael, the great prince who stands guard over the sons of your people, will arise." (NAS)

The word "great prince" we can interpret as "archangel." This particular archangel, Michael, stands guard over the sons of Daniel's people, the children of Israel.

Michael, in some special way, is charged by God with watching over the interests and protecting Israel. Because this whole revelation centered around the future of Israel, it was very much in the interests of Israel that the messenger should get through. So when the first angel was held up, then the archangel Michael came to help him and they battled there with the satanic angels for twenty-one days.

The satanic angels were represented by one who was known as the prince of the kingdom of Persia (the supreme ruler) and under him various kings or subordinate rulers who had various areas of authority. For instance, there might be one king over each major city of the Persian Empire, one over each major ethnic group, perhaps one also over each of the various religious and pagan cults of the Persian Empire. We get a picture of a highly organized, structured kingdom with various areas and descending levels of authority with headquarters in the heavenlies and which is a kingdom of rebellious, fallen spirit-beings.

The angel again speaks about this conflict in Daniel 10:20:

> 20 . . . "Do you understand why I came to you? But I shall now return to fight against the prince of Persia. . . ." (NAS)

In other words, the battle against this evil satanic angel that dominated the empire of Persia was not yet complete. There would be further war in the heavens. The angel continues:

> 20 ". . . I am going forth, and behold, the prince of Greece is about to come." (NAS)

In other words, once victory has been gained over the evil angel that rules the empire of Persia, the next empire that will arise will be the empire of Greece and that also will have its own specific evil angel that is the ruler, or prince, of Greece.

In verse 21, the angel that is speaking to Daniel says:

> 21 "Yet there is no one who stands firmly with me against these forces except Michael your prince." (NAS)

So we see again that the archangel Michael is specifically associated with protecting and watching over the interests of God's people, Israel. We also see that it took the united strength of the first angel and Michael to overcome the satanic ruling angels in Satan's kingdom that were opposing the outworking of God's purpose for Israel.

You might wonder at the reference to Persia and Greece. Let me remind you that there were four major Gentile empires that successively dominated Israel and the city of Jerusalem from about the fifth century B.C. and onwards. They were Babylon, Persia, Greece, and Rome. Persia and Greece were significant because, at that time, they were the two dominant Gentile empires.

We see from these passages in Daniel that the battle centers around God's people and God's purposes. I believe that is still true today. Wherever God's people are and God's purposes are being worked out, that is where the spiritual battle will be most intense. In my opinion, in the days in which we now live, the center of the conflict is once again over Israel and the city of Jerusalem.

The effect of Daniel's prayers is somewhat staggering. When Daniel started to pray on earth it set all heaven in motion, both the angels of God and the angels of Satan. That gives us a terrific insight into what prayer can do.

I am also impressed by the fact that God's angels apparently needed the help of Daniel's prayers to get them through and accomplish their mission. Again, that gives us a tremendous insight into the effectiveness of prayer.

Chapter 4

The Weapons and the Battleground

We will now look at two related aspects of spiritual warfare. First, the weapons which we must use. Second, the battleground on which the war is fought. Both are revealed in 2 Corinthians 10:3-5. First, the American Standard Version says:

> 3 For though we walk in the flesh, we do not war according to the flesh,
> 4 for the weapons of our warfare are not of the flesh. . . .　　　　　(NAS)

Notice, Paul says we are living in the flesh, engaged in a war, but our war is not in the fleshly realm. Therefore, the weapons we use must correspond to the nature of the war. If the nature of the war were fleshly or physical, then we could use fleshly or physical weapons, such as tanks, bombs, or bullets. Because the war is spiritual and in a spiritual realm, the weapons also must be spiritual.

> 4 . . . for the weapons of our warfare are
> not of the flesh, but divinely powerful for
> the destruction of fortresses.
> 5 We are destroying speculations and every
> lofty thing raised up against the knowledge
> of God, and we are taking every thought
> captive to the obedience of Christ. . . .
>
> (NAS)

Notice, our weapons are appropriate to the war, and we are dealing with fortresses.

The King James version reads:

> 3 For though we walk in the flesh, we do
> not war after the flesh:
> 4 (For the weapons of our warfare are not
> carnal [fleshly or physical], but mighty
> through God to the pulling down of strong
> holds;)
> 5 Casting down imaginations, and every
> high thing that exalteth itself against the
> knowledge of God, and bringing into
> captivity every thought to the obedience of
> Christ. . . .   (KJV)

Where the New American Standard says "fortresses" the King James says "strongholds."

The warfare is in the spiritual realm; therefore, the weapons are spiritual and appropriate to the realm of the warfare. These weapons will be my main theme in the two following sections, "Our Defensive Armor" and "Weapons of Attack."

It is tremendously important that we understand where the battle is taking place. Speaking of the battleground and our objectives, Paul uses various words. I will choose from various different translations the following words: imaginations, reasonings, speculations, arguments, knowledge and thought. Notice that every one of those words refers to the same particular realm, the realm of the mind. We **absolutely must understand the battleground is in the realm of the mind.** Satan is waging an all out war to captivate the minds of the human race. He is building strongholds and fortresses in their minds and it is our responsibility, as God's representatives, to use our spiritual weapons to break down these strongholds, to liberate the minds of men and women, and then to bring them into captivity to the obedience of Christ. What a staggering assignment that is!

Satan deliberately and systematically builds strongholds in people's minds. These strongholds and fortresses resist the truth of the gospel and the Word of God and prevent people from being able to receive the message of the gospel.

What kind of strongholds does the Bible indicate? I would suggest two fairly common English words that describe the type of strongholds in people's minds. These are prejudices and preconception.

Maybe you have heard this definition: "Prejudice is being down on what you are not up on." In other words, if you know nothing about it, it is sure to be wrong. If you were not the first to think of it, then it is dangerous. If ever that was true of any group of people, it is true of religious people. Almost anything about which religious people have not heard, they view with intense fear and suspicion.

There is another example of prejudice which is contained in the famous statement, "Don't confuse me with the facts, my mind is made up!" That is prejudice. When a person's mind is already made up in advance, no amount of facts, truth, evidence or reason can change it. Only spiritual weapons can break down those strongholds. People are driven and dominated by prejudices and preconceptions, often to their own destruction. One example really impressed me, maybe because I am English by background.

In the American Revolutionary War, the soldiers were fighting the American rebels. The

English idea of war was to put on full highly-colored uniforms and march in rank with the drums rolling, into battle. The American sharpshooters just hid in the trees and swamps and simply shot these people down without ever being seen. By our standards today, that would be considered military suicide. In that time, however, people could not conceive of fighting in any other way. It was a stronghold of prejudice and preconception that caused the unnecessary death of thousands of English soldiers. This is just one example of how a mental prejudice can drive people to their own destruction.

There are other examples of prejudices that grip people's minds, such as religious cults, political ideologies, and racial prejudices. These are found, frequently, among professing Christians.

Some little while back, I was preaching in South Africa. I was asked to preach on the theme of principalities and spiritual warfare. As I meditated on it, the Lord seemed to give me the identity of the strong man over South Africa. It is bigotry. I looked up the word "bigot" in the dictionary and this was the definition: "One who holds, irrespective of reason, and attaches disproportionate weight to some creed or view." That is a bigot. It is also a stronghold. It is something Satan builds in people's minds.

After I had given this talk, a minister who was born in South Africa and knew the country well, said to me, "You couldn't have described the problems of South Africa any better. South Africa is riddled with bigotry; religious, racial, and denominational. The root problem of this nation is bigotry." South Africans, individually, are a most delightful group of people, but their minds have been captivated and held by this stronghold of bigotry. I am not suggesting that South Africans are different from other people, they just have their own particular kind of stronghold. 2 Corinthians 4:4 states:

> 4 The god of this age has blinded the minds
> of unbelievers, so that they cannot see the
> light of the gospel of the glory of Christ,
> who is the image of God. (NIV)

A stronghold is something that **blinds men's minds so that the light of the gospel cannot shine in.** When a person is in that condition, it is worse than useless to argue with him or her. The more you argue, the more they restate their error and the more firmly they are stuck in that error. The only way to deliver such people is to use our spiritual deliver such people is to use our spiritual weapons and break down the strongholds in their minds.

Chapter 5

The Basis of Our Victory

I will now explain the most important single fact that we must know in order to be assured of victory in our spiritual warfare. In Colossians 2:13-15, Paul describes what God has done for us, as believers, through the death of Christ on the cross on our behalf.

> 13 When you were dead in your sins and in the uncircumcision of your sinful nature, God made you alive with Christ. He forgave us all our sins,
> 14 having canceled the written code, with its regulations, that was against us and that stood opposed to us; he took it away, nailing it to the cross.
> 15 And having disarmed the powers and authorities, he made a public spectacle of them, triumphing over them by the cross.
>
> (NIV)

Let me first warn you that Satan is extremely determined that you shall not grasp this fact. He wants to keep all Christians from understanding it, because it is the key to his defeat. The great essential fact is this: **Christ has already defeated Satan and all his evil powers and authorities totally and forever.**

If you remember nothing else, remember that. **Christ has already defeated Satan and all his evil powers and authorities totally and forever.** He did that through His death on the cross, through His shed blood, and through His triumphant resurrection.

To understand how this was accomplished, we must recognize Satan's primary weapon against us, and that weapon is guilt. Revelation 12:10 states:

> 10 Then I heard a loud voice in heaven say: "Now have come the salvation and the power and the kingdom of our God, and the authority of his Christ. For the accuser of our brothers, who accuses them before our God day and night, has been hurled down." (NIV)

Who is the "accuser of the brothers?" We know that is Satan. I have already pointed out that Satan has access to the presence of God and his chief occupation is to accuse us who believe in Jesus.

Why does Satan accuse us? What is his objective? It can be stated in one simple phrase: to make us feel guilty. So long as Satan can keep us feeling guilty, we cannot defeat him. Guilt is the key to our defeat and righteousness is the key to our victory.

God, through the cross, has dealt with this problem of guilt, both in the past and in the future. He has made complete provision for both. How did God deal with the past? Colossians 2:13 says, "He forgave us all our sins. . . . " (NIV)

Through the death of Jesus Christ on our behalf, as our representative, carrying our guilt and paying our penalty, God is now able to forgive us for all our sinful acts. Because His justice has been satisfied by the death of Christ, He can forgive every sin we have ever committed without compromising His own justice. The first thing we must understand is that all our past sinful acts, no matter how many or how serious, have been forgiven when we put our faith in Jesus.

Then God made provision for the future, as shown in Colossians 2:14:

> 14 . . . having canceled the written code, with its regulations, that was against us

41

and that stood opposed to us; he took it
away, nailing it to the cross.   (NIV)

The "written code" is the law of Moses.
Jesus, on the cross, did away with the law of
Moses as a requirement for obtaining
righteousness with God. As long as the law of
Moses was the requirement, every time we
broke even one of the most minor
requirements, we were guilty before God. But
when the law was taken out of the way as a
requirement for achieving righteousness, then
provision was made for us to live free from
guilt because our **faith** is reckoned to us for
righteousness.

There are two related passages. One of these is
Romans 10:4:

4 For Christ is the end of the law for
righteousness to everyone who believes.
                            (NAS)

That is an important statement. Jew or
Gentile, Catholic or Protestant, it makes no
difference. Christ is not the end of the law as
part of God's Word, or as a part of the history
of Israel, or in any other aspect. He is the end
of the law as a means to achieve righteousness
with God. We are not required to keep the law
in order to be righteous.

The second relevant Scripture is 2 Corinthians 5:21:

> 21 God made him who had no sin [Jesus] to be sin for us, so that in him we might become the righteousness of God.   (NIV)

That is the divine exchange. Jesus was made sin with our sinfulness that we might be made righteous with His righteousness. Once we grasp the fact that we have been made righteous with the righteousness of Christ, then the devil cannot make us feel guilty any longer. Satan's main weapon will thus be taken from him. Jesus disarmed the principalities and powers by His death on the cross. He took from them their main weapon against us.

Now I want to show you the outworking of Christ's victory through us. We have already seen the statement of Christ's victory in Colossians 2:15:

> 15 And having disarmed the powers and authorities [Satan's whole evil kingdom], he made a public spectacle of them, triumphing over them by the cross. (NIV)

A triumph is not actually the winning of a victory, it is the celebration and demonstration of a victory that has already been won. Jesus, through His death on the cross, demonstrated to the whole universe His victory over the entire satanic kingdom. However, Jesus did not win that victory for Himself, He did not need it. He won it for us. It is God's purpose that that victory should be worked out and demonstrated through us. In 2 Corinthians 2:14 (one of my favorite verses), Paul says:

> 14 But thanks be to God, who always leads us in His triumph in Christ and manifests through us the sweet aroma of the knowledge of Him in every place.   (NAS)

No wonder Paul says, "thanks be to God." Thanking God could not be helped if you really grasped the message of that verse. God always causes us to share Christ's triumph over Satan's kingdom. There are two adverbial phrases, "always" and "in every place." That means there is no time and no place when we cannot visibly share the triumph of Christ over Satan's kingdom.

In Matthew 28:18-20, Jesus declares:

> 18 Then Jesus came to them and said, "All authority in heaven and on earth has been given to me.
> 19 "Therefore go and make disciples of all nations, baptizing them in the name of the Father and of the Son and of the Holy Spirit,

20 "and teaching them to obey everything
I have commanded you. And surely I will be
with you always, to the very end of the
age." (NIV)

Here Jesus says that through His death on the
cross, He has wrested the authority from
Satan, obtained it for Himself, and God has
vested in Him all authority in heaven and
earth. Then He says, "Therefore go and make
disciples. . . ." What is the implication of the
"therefore?" Jesus says, "I have won the
authority, you go and exercise it. You go and
demonstrate My victory to the whole world by
fulfilling My commission."

I would now like to make three simple
statements about the victory of Jesus. First, in
the wilderness temptation, Jesus defeated
Satan on His own behalf. He met Satan,
resisted his temptation, and defeated him.
Second, on the cross, Jesus defeated Satan on
our behalf, not for Himself, but for us. He did
not need the victory for Himself because He
already had it, but He won the victory for us
and defeated our enemy. He disarmed our
enemy, stripped him, and made a show of him
openly on our behalf. Third, it is now our
responsibility to demonstrate and administer
the victory of Jesus.

14 But thanks be to God, who always leads us in His triumph in Christ and manifests through us the sweet aroma of the knowledge of Him in every place.

(2 Corinthians 2:14 NAS)

Remember that "always" and "in every place" Christ has made victory possible for us.

Part 2:

OUR DEFENSIVE ARMOR

Chapter 6

The Full Armor of God

I have already explained that as the representatives of God's kingdom here on earth, we find ourselves involved in an all-out war with a highly-organized opposing kingdom ruled by Satan. This is a kingdom of evil spirit-beings (persons without bodies) whose headquarters are in the heavenly realms.

The battleground on which this war is being fought is the minds of humanity. Satan has built up strongholds of prejudice and unbelief in the minds of the human race to keep them from receiving the truth of the gospel. Our God given task is to break down these mental strongholds, thus releasing men and women from Satan's deception, and then bring them into submission and obedience to Christ.

Our ability to achieve this God-given task depends mainly upon two factors. First, that we see clearly from Scripture that on the cross Jesus totally defeated Satan on our behalf and that it is now our responsibility to demonstrate and administer the victory which Jesus has already won. Second, that we make proper use of the necessary spiritual weapons with which God has provided us. These spiritual weapons fall into two main categories: weapons of defense and weapons of attack. In this section, we will deal with the first category, weapons of defense.

Ephesians 6:10-17 is our basis:

10 Finally, be strong in the Lord, and in the strength of His might.
11 Put on the full armor of God, that you may be able to stand firm against the schemes of the devil.
12 For our struggle is not against flesh and blood, but against the rulers, against the powers, against the world forces of this darkness, against the spiritual forces of wickedness in the heavenly places.
13 Therefore, take up the full armor of God, that you may be able to resist in the evil day, and having done everything, to stand firm.
14 Stand firm therefore, having girded your loins with truth, and having put on the breastplate of righteousness,
15 and having shod your feet with the preparation of the gospel of peace;
16 in addition to all, taking up the shield of faith with which you will be able to

extinguish all the flaming missiles of the
evil one.
17 And take the helmet of salvation, and
the sword of the Spirit, which is the word of
God.   (NAS)

Early in that passage Paul says, "Therefore,
take up the full armor of God. . . ." We are
dealing with taking up the full armor of God.
You may have heard me comment before that
whenever you find a "therefore" in the
Bible, you want to find out what it is "there
for." The "therefore" in this verse is there
because of the preceding verse where Paul
says, ". . . our struggle is not against flesh
and blood, but against the rulers, against the
powers, against the world forces of this
darkness, against the spiritual forces of
wickedness in the heavenlies." It is because
we are involved in this life-and-death struggle
with the evil spirit forces of Satan's kingdom
that we owe it to ourselves (and God's Word
requires it of us), to put on the full armor of
God. It is significant that twice in this passage
(v. 11 and 13) Paul says, "Put on the full
armor of God." Surely, we have been clearly
warned by Scripture that we must protect
ourselves with the full armor of God.

In verse 13 Paul gives a further reason, "that
you may be able to resist in the evil day, and
having done everything, to stand firm."

51

Notice the phrase, "the evil day." I do not believe this means the Great Tribulation or some prophetic disaster that is going to come on the world (although I do believe there may be such disasters). I believe in that context "the evil day" refers to something that every Christian will go through. This will be a time when he must confront the forces of evil, where his faith is going to be challenged, and where every kind of opposition and problem will be loosed against him.

Paul does not question our need to face the evil day. It is not an option but a certainty. I always think of the parable Jesus gave concerning the two men who built houses. The foolish man built on sand, and the wise man built on rock. The foolish man's house collapsed, but the wise man's house stood. The difference between those two houses was not the tests to which they were subjected because each house was subjected to the same test: the wind, the rain, the storm and the flood. The difference was the foundation on which they were built.

Nothing in the Scripture indicates that we, as Christians, will escape these tests. We will not escape "the evil day," we must be prepared to go through it. In the light of this, Paul says, "Put on the whole armor of God."

Paul takes his picture from a Roman legionary of his day and lists six pieces of equipment that a legionary would normally wear. Let me list them for you:

> First, the girdle of truth;
>
> Second, the breastplate of righteousness;
>
> Third, the shoes of the preparation of the gospel;
>
> Fourth, the shield of faith;
>
> Fifth, the helmet of salvation;
>
> Sixth, the sword of the Spirit.

You will understand, as you meditate on that, that if you put on all these six pieces of equipment, you will be fully protected from the crown of your head to the soles of your feet with one exception. There is no protection for the back. I will cover that at the end of this section.

Chapter 7

The Girdle of Truth

The first item of equipment is the girdle of truth. We must understand why a Roman legionary would need a girdle as part of his equipment. Remember that in those days, men's clothing (as well as women's) was usually a loose garment that came at least to the knees. In the case of the Roman legionary, it was a kind of tunic. When a Roman legionary was required to do something active, such as fight or use his weapons, he would need to take care of that loose garment. If he did not, its flaps and folds would hinder his movements and prevent him from using the rest of his equipment effectively.

The first thing he had to do was to tie his girdle tightly around his waist in such a way that the tunic no longer flapped freely and could not hinder his further movements. This was essential and it was the basis for everything else. That is why Paul mentions the girdle of truth before he speaks about anything else.

Quite often the Bible speaks about a man "girding up his loins." This is what is meant by that phrase.

Paul says the girdle for us is truth. I believe that does not mean abstract, theological truth, but truth in daily living. It means honesty, sincerity, openness, and frankness.

As religious people, we are often encumbered with much sham and hypocrisy. Many things we say and do are not really meant, but we say them only because they sound good. We are full of religious cliches and insincerities. There are things we do, not to please God or because we really want to do them, but to please other people. Almost every religious group has its own particular cliches like, "Jesus will help you, brother." Sometimes that is nothing but a "cop-out," because it is not Jesus who needs to help your brother, it is YOU who needs to help your brother.

Religious talk like that is just like a loose, hanging garment. It gets in our way and prevents us from doing the kind of thing that God asks us to do. It prevents us from being active, energetic, effective Christians. It also prevents us from using the other items of equipment.

We are required, first of all, to put on the girdle of truth. We must put away sham, hypocrisy, religious cliches, and saying and doing things we do not mean.

Often truth is quite painful. You must begin to show other people the kind of person you really are. You may have been hiding away or putting on a religious front all this time and now you are confronted with the need for real truth, openness and frankness. You must put on the girdle and tie it around so that these religious insincerities and shams no longer hang around you and get in the way of things God is asking you to do.

Chapter 8

The Breastplate of Righteousness

The breastplate of the Roman legionary protects, above all else, one absolutely vital organ of the human body: the heart. The Bible indicates that the heart is of supreme importance in our lives as stated by Solomon in Proverbs 4:23:

> 23 Watch over your heart with all diligence,
> For from it flow the springs of life. (NAS)

I was a teacher in Kenya, East Africa, for five years. I became acquainted with a number of the tribes and learned a little of their languages. One day, on the wall of a student's dormitory, I saw Proverbs 4:23 quoted in the Maragoli language. I translated it to myself literally and I have always remembered the translation. "Guard your heart with all your strength for all the things there are in life come out of it."

What you have in your heart must ultimately determine the course of your life, for good or for evil. It is essential that we protect our heart from all kinds of evil. Paul speaks about the breastplate of righteousness as a protection of the heart.

We must ask ourselves what is meant by righteousness in this context. Fortunately, Paul returns to this theme of armor in another epistle. In 1 Thessalonians 5:8, he says this:

> 8 But since we are of the day, let us be sober, having put on the breastplate of faith and love. . . . (NAS)

Here Paul describes the breastplate from another point of view. He calls it "the breastplate of faith and love." Put these two passages together: "the breastplate of righteousness" is a "breastplate of faith and love." This tells us the kind of righteousness that Paul has in mind. It is not the righteousness of works, or religious law, but it is the righteousness that comes only by faith.

Paul speaks about this kind of righteousness again in Philippians 3:9:

> 9 . . . [that I] may be found in Him [Christ], not having a righteousness of my own derived from the Law, but that which is

through faith in Christ, the righteousness
which comes from God on the basis of faith.
. . .   (NAS)

Paul now puts the two kinds of righteousness
side by side. First of all, he speaks about a
righteousness of his own derived from the Law
and says this is not sufficient. As an
alternative, he speaks of the righteousness that
comes from God on the basis of faith. That is
the kind of righteousness which he has in mind
when he speaks about the breastplate of
righteousness that protects the heart. As long
as we are wearing a breastplate which is
simply our own righteousness, Satan can find
many weak points in that type of righteousness
and can often penetrate it with his attacks and
damage our heart. We must put on a
breastplate which is not our own righteousness
but the righteousness of Christ. 2 Corinthians
5:21 reads:

21 [God] made Him who knew no sin
[Jesus] to be sin on our behalf, that we
might become the righteousness of God in
Him [Christ].   (NAS)

We must be convinced out of Scripture and
accept by faith that we have become the
righteousness of God. That is the only kind of
breastplate that can adequately protect our
heart and our life.

61

This kind of righteousness, Paul emphasizes, comes only through faith. Therefore it is a breastplate of faith and love. There is no other way to achieve this kind of righteousness.

I am always moved by the prayer of Jesus for Peter on the night before His passion, when Jesus warned Peter that he was going to betray Him the same night. In the context of that warning, Jesus said, "Peter, I have prayed for you." Jesus did not pray that Peter would not betray Him. In those circumstances, under the pressures that would develop and with the known weaknesses in Peter's character, it was inevitable that Peter would betray Jesus. But Jesus prayed a different kind of prayer, the only prayer that could really help Peter. Jesus said in Luke 22:31-32:

> 31 "Simon, Simon, Satan has asked to sift you as wheat.
> 32 "But I have prayed for you, Simon, that your faith may not fail." (NIV)

Notice, "that your faith may not fail." Even though he was going to deny the Lord and show himself very weak and cowardly, everything could still be retrieved provided his faith did not fail. This is the breastplate of faith and love. Faith is the essential element for this breastplate.

The kind of faith that we are analyzing works only through love. Galatians 5:6 says:

> 6 For in Christ Jesus neither circumcision nor uncircumcision means anything, but faith working through love.   (NAS)

As I understand it, what Paul is really saying is, "No kind of outward ceremony or ritual, in itself, is sufficient. The one essential thing, without which we cannot succeed in the Christian life, is faith, the kind of faith that works through love. It is not a passive or theoretical faith. It is an active faith that works only through love."

The more I meditate upon it, the more I am impressed by the irresistible power of love. I love the passage in Song of Solomon 8:6-7:

> 6 Place me like a seal over your heart, like a seal over your arm; for love is as strong as death,
> 7 Many waters cannot quench love; rivers cannot wash it away.   (NIV)

Think of the statement "love is as strong as death." Death is the one irresistible thing that we all must encounter. There is not one of us that can resist it. There is no way to avoid it. Scripture says that love is as strong as death.

Think about it. Love is irresistible. It always conquers. There is no way it can be defeated. Love protects us from all negative forces like resentment, unforgiveness, bitterness, discouragement, and despair which can corrupt our hearts and spoil our lives. Remember, all that there is in life comes out of the heart.

Paul describes this kind of love in 1 Corinthians 13:4-8:

> 4 Love is patient, love is kind. It does not envy, it does not boast, it is not proud.
> 5 It is not rude, it is not self-seeking, it is not easily angered, it keeps no record of wrongs.
> 6 Love does not delight in evil but rejoices with the truth.
> 7 It always protects, always trusts, always hopes, always perseveres.
> 8 Love never fails. (NIV)

That is the breastplate we need, one that never fails. A breastplate in which there are no weak points that Satan can penetrate. What Paul says there is so appropriate to the picture of the breastplate. Love always protects, always trusts, always hopes, always perseveres. When you have on that breastplate of faith that works by love, it will always protect you. It will keep your heart from every attack and attempt of Satan to penetrate that vital area of your life.

Chapter 9

The Shoes of the Preparation of the Gospel

The shoes Roman legionaries usually wore were strong, heavy sandals with thongs to keep them in place. They usually laced at least half-way up the calf with leather thongs. They were a very important part of the legionary's equipment because they enabled him to march long distances at speed. This gave him mobility. It made him available to his commander at the time and the place where he was needed in the battle. Think of shoes as providing mobility and availability to your commander, the Lord Jesus Christ. This became very real to me in my own personal experience.

For two years during World War II, I served with a hospital unit with the British Army in the deserts of North Africa. There were times while we were working with an armored division that we were very close to the enemy lines, sometimes at night. In the desert it is not easy to know exactly where the enemy lines are because the whole war is very mobile. In such situations, our commanding officer always gave orders that we were not to take our boots off at night. We were to sleep with our boots on. Of course, the reason is obvious. You are usually not at your best when you wake out of sound sleep. If you do not have your boots on and there is confusion all around you, you can spend several valuable minutes groping in the dark for your boots, then trying to put them on and lace them up. If, however, you have your boots on, you are instantly available. The key is availability or mobility.

This is also true of the spiritual counterpart of our equipment about which Paul speaks. The shoes, or the sandals, are called "the preparation of the gospel." In other words, it means being ready with something. As Christians, we are obligated to have an intelligent understanding of the gospel. Many Christians claim to be saved and born again but they cannot give an intelligent account of how they were saved or how someone else can be saved. I believe "preparation" includes study of the Scripture, memorization of Scripture, and the ability to communicate intelligently the gospel message. Notice also that Paul calls it "the gospel of peace." It is a gospel that produces peace of heart and mind in those who believe it and obey it.

There is one thing very certain about peace. We can only transmit peace to others if we have peace ourselves. We cannot transmit something that we do not experience. We can talk about it, we can theorize, but we cannot transmit it.

There is a very significant passage in Matthew 10:12-13, where Jesus gave instructions to the first disciples when He sent them out for the first time to preach the gospel. This is part of His instruction:

> 12 As you enter the home, give it your greeting.
> 13 If the home is deserving, let your peace rest on it; if it is not, let your peace return to you.   (NIV)

Notice that significant phrase, if a home is deserving, "let your peace rest on it. . . ." You are to impart your peace to it. When you go into a home, do you have peace to impart? You cannot impart something that you are not enjoying yourself.

Let me give you a little example of how this might work. Suppose you are a lady doing your grocery shopping in a supermarket. As you wait in the check-out line, there is a lady who is obviously on the verge of a nervous breakdown. She is nervous and jittery and God directs you to help her. What are you going to do? Are you going to say, "Come to church on Sunday morning?" That will not meet her need. If that was all you could say, you would not have your shoes on.

Having your shoes on means you are ready to do something right then and there when God directs you. First of all, you must have peace. You must let her feel that you have something that she does not have and desperately needs. People can feel peace in other people.

When she reaches out for that peace, you must be able to tell her in simple, nonreligious language just how she can find peace. You must be able to communicate the gospel to her. That is the "shoes of the preparation of the gospel of peace."

Chapter 10

The Shield of Faith

In the Greek of the New Testament, there are two different words for "shield." One is a small, circular shield, shaped more or less like a large, round flat wicker basket. The other one is a long rectangular shield and is taken from the word for a door because it is shaped somewhat like a door. This is the kind of shield Paul speaks of when he says "the shield of faith."

A properly trained Roman legionary could use that shield so that no part of his body could be reached by the missiles of the enemy. It protected him completely. This is the kind of faith Paul is speaking about when he refers to it as a shield.

When we go out against Satan, if we begin to cause him any trouble, you can be sure he will counterattack. First, he may counterattack our minds, our hearts, our bodies, or our finances, so we need to have a shield that covers us. He will attack any area he can reach. If he cannot attack us, he will attack those closest to us. If you are a married man, the first thing that Satan will attack is your wife. It is almost to be guaranteed. That is one of the ways he will get back at you. You must have a shield big enough to protect everything for which God has made you responsible, including yourself, your family, and everything God has committed to you. I once learned this lesson in a very vivid way.

I was ministering once to a woman who had a demon of suicide. At a certain point, she received a very definite, dramatic deliverance, and she knew she was free. We both praised God. The next day she came back to see me and related this remarkable incident. She said that just about the time she received her deliverance, her husband was driving along the highway in his open pick-up truck and their German Shepherd dog was standing (as the dog always loved to do) in the back of the truck. For no reason, while the truck was traveling at high speed, the shepherd dog suddenly jumped out and was instantly killed.

The moment she told me that, I understood that the demon of suicide which had left the woman had gone into the dog. Satan attacked the nearest thing he could reach. I learned a lesson I trust I will never need to learn again.

Whenever I minister deliverance to people, I always claim the protection of faith in the blood of Jesus over everything that is connected with them. Nothing like that has ever happened to me again. This taught me the importance of the shield of faith as a great, door-shaped shield that protects everything God has committed to us.

Faith is mentioned twice in this list of the armor. The breastplate is faith and love and the shield is the shield of faith. Each use of "faith" must be understood slightly differently. The breastplate is faith for our own personal righteousness, but the shield is faith for protection and provision for ourselves and all whom God has committed to us. It is that which covers everything.

I learned this in a vivid way at the beginning of my radio ministry. When I got launched into this ministry, it was remarkable how many things simultaneously went wrong in the office and in production. Equipment that should have functioned perfectly suddenly ceased to function. Personnel became sick, messages went astray. Confusion broke loose in our usually well-ordered organization. Then I realized I was required to stretch out the shield of faith. Satan was counterattacking and he could not reach me, personally, so he attacked something that I depended upon, those who supported my ministry. But I held out the shield of faith, rebuked that power of confusion, and peace and order were restored. Once again, I learned a lesson. We must hold out a shield of faith for full protection and provision.

Chapter 11

The Helmet of Salvation

The fifth item of equipment is the helmet of salvation. I will share some precious truths concerning this that I learned from my own conflicts.

When I look back on these conflicts, I am reminded of the words of Paul in Romans 8:37:

> 37 No, in all these things we are more than conquerors through him who loved us.
>
> (NIV)

What does it mean to be more than conquerors? It means we not only win the battle but actually come out of it with more than we had when we went into it. I have proved this many times in my own experience.

In dealing with the breastplate, we saw that the breastplate protects the heart. Now that we are looking at the helmet, we can see that it protects the head and that the head represents the mind. In effect, we are talking about a helmet which protects our minds.

We saw previously that the battlefield on which this entire spiritual war is being fought is the mind of humanity. Because the mind is the battlefield, it is obvious that we need to be particularly careful to protect our own minds.

As a hospital attendant in World War II, I became aware of this from experience. In the natural, a person wounded in the head can no longer make effective use of the rest of his equipment. He may be a very brave and efficient soldier and have excellent equipment, but when he is wounded in the head, it becomes very difficult for him to make effective use of his ability and his equipment.

In the spiritual, this is true of many Christian workers. I have been privileged to be associated in ministry at different times and in different places with many wonderful servants of God, both men and women. I think particularly of missionaries, who are usually under extreme spiritual pressure. Some missionaries that I worked with were dedicated, qualified men and women of God, with great ability and a real calling. Many times, however, they allowed themselves to be wounded in the head. By this I mean that they allowed themselves to become prey to depression or to mistrust other Christian workers. This problem in their minds prevented them from being the kind of effective missionaries and servants of God that they could have been. Being wounded in the head, they could not use the rest of their equipment.

In my own experience, I had a tremendous personal struggle with depression for many years. It was like a dark gray cloud or mist that settled down over me, shut me in, shut me off, and made it difficult for me to communicate with others. It gave me a sense of hopelessness and, although in many ways I am a gifted and qualified servant of the Lord, I got the impression, "Others can, but you can't. You'll never make it. You're going to have to give up."

I struggled with this depression for a good many years. I did everything I could. I prayed, I fasted, I sought God, I read the Bible. Then one day God gave me a revelation that solved my problem. I was reading Isaiah 61:3:

> 3 To appoint unto them that mourn in Zion,
> to give unto them beauty for ashes, the oil

of joy for mourning, the garment of praise
for the spirit of heaviness. . . . (KJV)

When I read that phrase, "the spirit of
heaviness," something leaped within me. I
said, "That's my problem! That's what I need
to be delivered from." I read other passages
of Scripture on deliverance, I prayed a simple
prayer of faith, and God supernaturally
delivered me from that spirit of heaviness.

I then saw that I needed some special
protection for my mind. I was familiar with the
passage in Ephesians 6. I said to myself,
"That must be the helmet of salvation."

Then I said, "Does that mean I have the
helmet because I'm saved? Is it automatic?"
I saw that could not be so because Paul was
writing to people who were Christians when he
said, "put on the helmet of salvation." I was
directed to a parallel passage in 1 Thessalonians 5:8:

> 8 But let us, who are of the day, be sober,
> putting on the breastplate of faith and love;
> and for an helmet, the hope of salvation.
>   (KJV)

And when I read that phrase, "the hope of
salvation," I had an instantaneous revelation

from the Holy Spirit. I saw that the protection for the mind is hope, but the protection for the heart is faith. We often get these mixed up. Biblical faith is in the heart: "With the heart man believeth unto righteousness." Biblical faith is the breastplate that protects the heart. But the protection of the mind is hope.

We need to see the connection between faith and hope. It is stated clearly in Hebrews 11:1:

> 1 Now faith is the substance of things hoped for. . . .   (KJV)

Faith is the underlying basic reality on which hope is built. When we have valid faith, then we have valid hope. When we do not have valid faith, we may not have valid hope either. Hope may be mere wishful thinking. But when we have a real foundation of faith, we can build a valid hope which is the protection of our mind.

I would like to define hope, very simply, according to Scripture. Hope is a quiet, steady expectation of good based on the promises of God's Word. In a sense, it is continuing optimism. That is the protection of the mind. Hope is an optimistic attitude that always chooses to see the best and will not give way to depression, doubt, and self-pity.

There is one sufficient basis for hope in the Word of God in Romans 8:28:

> 28 And we know that God causes all things to work together for good to those who love God, to those who are called according to His purpose. (NAS)

If we really know that everything that happens in our lives is being worked together by God for our good, then there never is a reason for pessimism. Every situation is always a reason for optimism. Optimism is the helmet. While we keep it on, our minds are protected against all Satan's subtle attacks of doubt, discouragement, self-pity, mistrust, and so on.

When the Holy Spirit showed me that the helmet to protect our mind is hope, He preached a kind of sermon to me. I suddenly brought together a number of passages in the New Testament all dealing with hope. Let me share just a few of them. Romans 8:24 reads:

> 24 For we are saved by hope. . . . (KJV)

What does that mean? No hope, no salvation. Hope is an essential part of our salvation experience. Contrast the condition of the unsaved in Ephesians 2:12:

> 12 [Before you knew Christ] . . . ye were without Christ, being aliens from the commonwealth of Israel, and strangers from the covenants of promise, having no hope, and without God in the world. . . . (KJV)

Being without Christ, without hope, and without God is the condition of the lost. It should never be the condition of the Christian. If we have Christ, then we have hope and we have God. Colossians 1:2 states:

> 27 . . . to whom God willed to make known what is the riches of the glory of this mystery among the Gentiles, which is Christ in you, the hope of glory. (NAS)

The real mystery, the secret of the gospel, is "Christ in you." If Christ is in you, you have hope. If you do not have hope, it is just as if Christ is not in you. You are not a lost soul, but I mean that you are not living in the experience of salvation. Hope in your mind is an essential part of your salvation experience. In Hebrews 6:17-20, there are two beautiful pictures of hope:

> 17 Because God wanted to make the unchanging nature of his purpose very clear

to the heirs of what was promised, he
confirmed it with an oath.
18 God did this so that, by two
unchangeable things in which it is
impossible for God to lie, we who have fled
to take hold of the hope offered to us may
be greatly encouraged.
19 We have this hope as an anchor for the
soul, firm and secure. It enters the inner
sanctuary behind the curtain,
20 where Jesus, who went before us, has
entered on our behalf.   (NIV)

The first picture of hope is an altar. Under the
Old Covenant, the altar was a place of
protection from the avengers of blood. When
you fled to the altar, you were safe. The writer
of Hebrews says that when all the pressures
are against us, flee to the altar, catch hold of
the horns of the altar and let nothing pull you
away. The altar is hope.

Second, hope is like an anchor that reaches out
of time into eternity, into the very presence of
God. In this world, we are like a little vessel on
the sea, everything around us is temporary,
impermanent, unreliable, changeable. There is
nothing to give us security and stability. If we
are to have security and stability we need an
anchor that reaches out of time into eternity
and fastens in the Rock of Ages. When we have
hope, we are anchored.

Finally, in Hebrews 10:23, we read:

> 23 Let us hold unswervingly to the hope we
> profess . . .   (NIV)

Keep on hoping. Do not give up hope, be an
optimist. It is the protection of your mind.

Chapter 12

The Sword of the Spirit

There is one thing that distinguishes the sword from the other five items that we have examined. The sword is the first item that is not purely defensive. Without it, we have no way to drive off the devil. If we put on all the other items of equipment, we may be able to prevent the devil from actually wounding us, but we cannot drive him from our presence. The only thing in that list that can do that is the sword, which is called "the Word of God."

The Bible compares God's Word to a sword because God's Word pierces and penetrates. Hebrews 4:12 declares:

> 12 The word of God is living and active. Sharper than any double-edged sword, it penetrates even to dividing soul and spirit, joints and marrow; it judges the thoughts and attitudes of the heart.   (NIV)

God's Word penetrates to every area of human personality. It penetrates to the marrow, the very innermost part of the physical being. It also penetrates and divides between soul and spirit, the innermost area of human personality. It is sharper than any double-edged sword.

In Revelation 1:16, where John had a vision of Jesus in His glory as the Lord of the church, one of the things that he saw was a sword coming out of the mouth of Jesus.

> 16 In his right hand he held seven stars, and out of his mouth came a sharp double-edged sword. (NIV)

That sharp double-edged sword is the Word of God coming out of the mouth of Jesus. Since it is indicated in Scripture that Jesus Himself uses the sword of the Word of God, we would do well to study just how Jesus used it in His earthly life. The clearest picture of this is found in Matthew 4:1-11, which describes the temptation of Jesus by Satan in the wilderness. Let me point out that every time Jesus encountered Satan personally, the only weapon He used against him was the sword of the Spirit, or the Word of God.

> 1 Then Jesus was led by the Spirit into the desert to be tempted by the devil.

2 After fasting forty days and forty nights, he was hungry.

3 The tempter came to him and said, "If you are the Son of God, tell these stones to become bread."

4 Jesus answered, "It is written: 'Man does not live on bread alone, but on every word that comes from the mouth of God.'"

5 Then the devil took him to the holy city and had him stand on the highest point of the temple.

6 "If you are the Son of God," he said, "throw yourself down. For it is written: 'He will command his angels concerning you, and they will lift you up in their hands, so that you will not strike your foot against a stone.'"

7 Jesus answered him, "It is also written: 'Do not put the Lord your God to the test.'"

8 Again, the devil took him to a very high mountain and showed him all the kingdoms of the world and their splendor.

9 "All this I will give you," he said, "if you will bow down and worship me."

10 Jesus said to him, "Away from me, Satan! For it is written: 'Worship the Lord your God, and serve him only.'"

11 Then the devil left him, and angels came and attended him. (Matthew 4:1-11 NIV)

I would like to point out some interesting things about that passage. First, neither Jesus nor Satan even questioned the authority of

Scripture. Isn't that remarkable? In particular, Jesus quoted each time from the book of Deuteronomy, the one book that has been singled out for attack by modern theologians and critics. Personally, I believe Jesus and Satan were wiser than the modern theologians. They both knew the authority of those words.

Second, the basis of every temptation against Jesus was a temptation to doubt. Every time Satan began with the word "if," he called something into doubt.

Third, as I have already indicated, Jesus did not vary His method of dealing with Satan, but always used the same weapon of the Word of God against him. "It is written . . . it is written . . . it is written. . ."

It is significant that the devil can quote Scripture, but he misapplies it. He quoted from Psalm 91, but Jesus quoted again from Deuteronomy. The devil tried to use Scripture against the Son of God. If he did it against Jesus, he might do it against you or me. We must know Scripture thoroughly and we must know how to apply Scripture if we are going to be able to handle the devil. We must be careful of people who misapply Scripture and try to tempt us to do the wrong thing.

Jesus did not answer the devil with theology or religious affiliation. He did not tell which synagogue He attended or which rabbi had taught Him. He always went straight to the Scripture. "It is written . . . it is written . . . it is written. . ." After the third thrust of that sharp double-edged sword, Satan backed off, he had had enough. You and I are given the privilege of using the same weapon.

In Ephesians 6:17, where Paul speaks about the sword of the Spirit, the Word of God, the Greek word he uses for "word" is *rhema,* which always primarily means a spoken word. It is significant that the sword of the Spirit is not the Bible on the bookshelf or on the nightstand. That does not scare the devil. But when you take the Scripture in your mouth and quote it directly, then it becomes the sword of the Spirit.

Notice also the significance of the phrase, "the sword of the Spirit." This indicates cooperation between the believer and the Holy Spirit. We must take the sword. The Holy Spirit will not do that for us. But when we take the sword in faith, then the Holy Spirit gives us the power and the wisdom to use it.

Chapter 13

The Unprotected Area

We have now covered all six items of protective armor. They are the girdle of truth, the breastplate of salvation, the shoes of the preparation of the gospel, the shield of faith, the helmet of salvation, and the sword of the Spirit, which is the Word of God. If we put on and use this entire protective equipment which God has provided, we are totally protected from the crown of our head to the soles of our feet, except for one area.

The one area for which there is no protection is our back. I believe this is very significant and has a twofold application. First, never turn your back on the devil because if you do you are giving him an opportunity to wound you in an unprotected area. In other words, never give up. Never turn around and say, "I've had enough. I can't stand this. I can't take anymore." That is turning your unprotected back to the devil and you can be sure he will avail himself of the opportunity to wound you.

Second, we are not always able to protect our own back. In the legions of Rome foot soldiers fought in close ranks. The Greek word for such a close rank was a *phalanx.* They were trained to fight this way and to never break rank. Every soldier knew the soldier on his right and on his left so that if he was being hard-pressed and could not protect his own back, there would be another soldier to do it for him.

I believe the same is true with us, as Christians. We cannot go out as isolated individuals and take on the devil's kingdom. We must come under discipline, find our place in the body (which is the army of Christ), and know who stands on our right and who stands on our left. We must be able to trust our fellow soldiers. Then, when we are under pressure, we ought to know who will be there to protect our back when we cannot protect it.

I have been in the ministry nearly forty years and have seen a great deal. The real tragedy of our Christian experience is that the very person who protects your back sometimes wounds you. How often we, as Christians, are wounded in the back by our fellow Christian. That is something which never ought to happen. Let us make up our minds to stand together, protect one another's back, and not wound one another.

Part 3:

WEAPONS OF ATTACK

Chapter 14

Taking the Offensive

We have dealt with the six items of defensive armor listed by Paul in Ephesians 6:14-17: the girdle of truth, the breastplate of righteousness, the shoes of the preparation of the gospel, the shield of faith, the helmet of salvation, and the sword of the Spirit. I pointed out that, with the exception of the sword, all these items are essentially for protection or self-defense. Even the sword can reach no further than the arm of the person who wields it. In other words, there is nothing in this list of defensive equipment that will enable us to deal with Satan's strongholds as Paul describes them in 2 Corinthians 10:4 and 5, where he speaks about our obligation to cast down Satan's strongholds or fortresses.

Now we want to move from the defensive to the offensive. We want to deal with weapons of attack that will enable us to assail and cast down Satan's strongholds. It is important that we see our obligation to take the offensive, to move out and actively attack Satan's kingdom.

It is a fact of history and experience that no army ever won a war on the defensive.

In the early part of this century, someone asked a well-known French general, "In a war, which army wins?" The general replied, "The one which advances."

That is probably an over-simplification, but at least it is true that we will never win a war by retreating or even by merely holding our ground. As long as Satan keeps the church on the defensive, his kingdom will never be overthrown. Therefore, we have an absolute obligation to move out from the defensive and from mere self-protection to an attack position.

When Jesus first unveiled His plan for the church, He envisioned it being on the offensive and attacking Satan's strongholds. The first time the word "church" is used in the New Testament is in Matthew 16:18. Jesus is here speaking to Peter, and He says this:

> 18 "You are Peter, a stone; and upon this rock I will build my church, and all the powers of hell shall not prevail against it." (TLB)

An alternative reading is "all the gates of hell shall not be too strong for it." The word for hell, in Greek, is the word, *hades*. The root meaning of the word *hades* is "invisible, unseen." So *hades*, or hell, is the unseen world of Satan's kingdom.

Jesus pictures His church in the light of two primary activities: building and battling. These must always go together. It is no good doing battle if we do not build. On the other hand, we cannot build if we do not battle. So we must think always in terms of building the church and battling the forces of Satan.

Many people have interpreted these words of Jesus incorrectly. They have somehow assumed that Jesus pictured the church on the defensive, being besieged in a city by Satan's forces. They have taken His promise to mean that Satan would not be able to batter the gate of that city down before Jesus came and caught the church away. That is really a totally defensive concept of the church in the world but it is completely incorrect.

Jesus pictures the church on the offensive, attacking the gates of Satan. Jesus promises that Satan's gates will not hold out against the church and that Satan will not be able to keep the church out. It is not the church trying to keep Satan out; it is Satan failing to keep the church out. Jesus promises us that, if we obey

Him as our commander-in-chief, we will be able to move out, storm Satan's citadels, break through his gates, release his captives, and carry away his spoil. That is the church's assignment, and it is essentially offensive, not defensive.

The word "gate" has a great deal of meaning in Scripture. First of all, the gate is the place of counsel and rule. For instance, in Proverbs 31:23, it says of the husband of the ideal wife, the faithful wife:

> 23 Her husband is respected at the city gate, where he takes his seat among the elders of the land. (NIV)

Notice the city gate was the place where the ruling council of elders sat and ruled and administered the city. So when the Scripture says that the gates of Satan will not prevail against the church, it means that Satan's councils will not prevail against the church but will be frustrated and brought to naught.

In attacking a city, the natural place to attack is the gates, because they are weaker than the walls. Isaiah 28:6 says:

> 6 A strength to those who repel the onslaught at the gate. (NAS)

The picture presented is the church making an onslaught on the gates of Satan's citadel and that the gates of Satan will not be able to keep the church out. So we must stop thinking on the defensive and start thinking on the offensive.

My experience is that most Christians have the attitude: "I wonder where the devil is going to strike next?" I suggest to you that the boot should be on the other foot. The devil should be wondering where the church is going to strike him next!

To continue with this theme of the church taking the offensive, I want to explain the scriptural basis for our doing so. It is found mainly in one verse, Colossians 2:15, which describes what God accomplished through the death of Christ on the cross on our behalf.

15 When He had disarmed the rulers and authorities. . . .   (NAS)

Now, the rulers and authorities are the same spiritual forces of Satan that are referred to in Ephesians 6:12. Through the cross, God disarmed those rulers and authorities. Have you ever thought that Satan has been left without armor? He has been stripped of his weapons. God, through the cross, disarmed the rulers and authorities. Then it says:

> 15 . . . He made a public display of them, having triumphed over them through Him. (Ephesians 6:15 NAS)

So God, through the cross, disarmed Satan's kingdom, He made a public display of the representatives of Satan's kingdom, and He triumphed over them in the cross.

A triumph is not so much winning a victory as it is the celebration of a victory that has already been won. It is a public demonstration that complete victory has been won.

On the cross, Jesus did not win the victory for Himself. He always had the victory. As our representative, He won the victory on our behalf. Thus His victory becomes our victory. 2 Corinthians 2:14 declares:

> 14 But thanks be to God, who always leads us in His triumph in Christ, and manifests through us the sweet aroma of the knowledge of Him in every place. (NAS)

"Always" and "in every place" we are to represent Christ's victory. God is going to demonstrate, publicly, the victory that Christ has won through us. That is the victory over

Satan's rulers and authorities or principalities and powers. This victory is to be worked out through us.

This is the final commission of Jesus, given to His disciples in Matthew 28:18-19:

> 18 And Jesus came up and spoke to them, saying, "All authority has been given to Me in heaven and on earth. [If Jesus has all authority, that leaves none for anybody else, except as He yields it.]
> 19 "Go therefore and make disciples of all the nations, baptizing them in the name of the Father and the Son and the Holy Spirit. . ." (NAS)

Jesus said, "All authority has already been given to Me. You go, therefore. . ." What does the "therefore" mean? I understand it to mean, "You go and exercise, on My behalf, the authority that I have already won." Our assignment is to administer the victory, demonstrate the triumph and exercise the authority that Jesus has won on our behalf. Authority is only effective when it is exercised. If we do not exercise the authority that He has given to us, it remains ineffective.

The world can only see Christ's victory when we demonstrate it. Christ has won the victory but our assignment is to demonstrate the victory over Satan and his kingdom, which Jesus has already won and this we can only do when we move from the defensive to the offensive.

Chapter 15

The Weapon of Prayer

In order that we may assail and cast down Satan's strongholds, God has provided us with appropriate spiritual weapons. 2 Corinthians 10:4 reads:

> 4 . . . for the weapons of our warfare are not of the flesh [they are not carnal, physical, or material; they are not bombs, bullets, tanks or war planes], but divinely powerful for the destruction of fortresses.
>
> (NAS)

Of course, that refers to Satan's fortresses. In other words, God has provided us with spiritual weapons. On the basis of much study and personal experience, I believe Scripture reveals four main spiritual weapons of attack. These are: prayer, praise, preaching, and testimony. We will consider first the weapon of prayer.

I must qualify this by saying that prayer is much more than a weapon. There are many different aspects to prayer, one being that

105

prayer is a weapon of spiritual warfare. I believe it is the most powerful of all the weapons that God has committed to us.

In Ephesians 6:18, after Paul listed the six items of defensive armor, he said:

> 18 And pray in the Spirit on all occasions
> with all kinds of prayers and requests.
> (NIV)

At that point He moved from the defensive to the offensive. It is no accident that that comes immediately after the list of defensive armor. He mentions there the greatest of all weapons of attack, which is prayer.

Think of prayer as an intercontinental ballistic missile. This is a missile that is launched from one continent, directed by an advanced guidance system to a target in a completely different continent to destroy an assigned target. There is no limitation of time or distance in prayer. Prayer is like that intercontinental ballistic missile. With it, we can assail Satan's strongholds anywhere, even in the heavenlies.

An example of a prayer of attack is related in Acts 12:1-6. The church had come under persecution by King Herod. James, one of the leaders, had already been executed by Herod. Now Peter was also arrested and was scheduled for execution shortly. This is the situation:

> 1 It was about this time that King Herod arrested some who belonged to the church, intending to persecute them.
> 2 He had James, the brother of John, put to death with the sword.
> 3 When he saw that this pleased the Jews, he proceeded to seize Peter also. This happened during the Feast of Unleavened Bread.
> 4 After arresting him, he put him in prison, handing him over to be guarded by four squads of four soldiers each. Herod intended to bring him out for public trial after the Passover. [He would not do it during the Passover because that would have been considered desecrating a holy period in the Jewish calendar.]
> 5 So Peter was kept in prison, but the church was earnestly praying to God for him.
> 6 The night before Herod was to bring him to trial, Peter was sleeping between two soldiers, bound with two chains, and sentries stood guard at the entrance.(NIV)

Peter was in the maximum security jail. Herod was so determined that no one rescue Peter that he actually had four squads of four soldiers each watching him night and day, four hours at a time. It is implied that one soldier was chained either to Peter's hands or feet. In the natural, any kind of rescue was totally impossible. The church, however, was earnestly praying.

A crisis adjusts our priorities. I do not know how earnestly the church had been in prayer, but suddenly James had been snatched from them. Now they saw the danger of Peter, their natural leader, being taken. That was motivation for earnest prayer. They were not only praying in the daytime, but the record indicates they were praying at night as well. It is important to notice that there are times when merely praying in the day will not be enough. Jesus said in Luke 18 that God would avenge His own elect who cried unto him day and night. There is an intensity in prayer that is sometimes needed to release God's intervention.

Jesus had given a promise to Peter in John 21:18-19:

> 18 "I tell you the truth, when you were younger you dressed yourself and went where you wanted; but when you are old you will stretch out your hands, and someone else will dress you and lead you where you do not want to go."

19 Jesus said this to indicate the kind of
death by which Peter would glorify God.
Then he said to him, "Follow me!"   (NIV)

I wonder whether Peter was meditating on that
promise in the prison. Jesus said, "when you
are old. . ." At that time, Peter was not yet
an old man. I suppose he must have reasoned
something was going to happen to cause the
word of Jesus to stand, and stand it did, but it
took the prayer of the church to make it
effective.

God answered the prayer of the church by
sending an angel to deliver Peter. Acts 12:8-11
states:

8 Then the angel said to him, "Put on
your clothes and sandals." And Peter did
so. "Wrap your cloak around you and
follow me," the angel told him.
9 Peter followed him out of the prison, but
he had no idea that what the angel was
doing was really happening; he thought he
was seeing a vision
10 They passed the first and second guards
and came to the iron gate leading to the
city. It opened for them by itself, and they
went through it. When they had walked
through the length of one street, suddenly
the angel left him.
11 Then Peter came to himself and said,
"Now I know without a doubt that the
Lord sent his angel and rescued me from

Herod's clutches and from everything the
Jewish people were anticipating." (NIV)

God answered the prayers of the church by
supernatural intervention through an angel.
However, the deliverance was only the first
part of the result of their prayer. We must also
see the second part, which was a judgment by
an angel on the persecutor, King Herod. In
Acts 12:19-23, we read:

> 19 After Herod had a thorough search made
> for him and did not find him, he
> cross-examined the guards and ordered that
> they be executed. Then Herod went from
> Judea to Caesarea and stayed there a
> while.
> 20 He had been quarreling with the people
> of Tyre and Sidon; they now joined together
> and sought an audience with him. Having
> secured the support of Blastus, a trusted
> personal servant of the king, they asked for
> peace, because they depended on the king's
> country for their food supply.
> 21 On the appointed day Herod, wearing
> his royal robes, sat on his throne and
> delivered a public address to the people.
> 22 They shouted, "This is the voice of a
> god, not of a man." [In other words, they
> flattered Herod by calling him a god. Notice
> the result.]
> 23 Immediately, because Herod did not give
> praise to God, an angel of the Lord struck
> him down, and he was eaten by worms and
> died.   (NIV)

Let us examine how prayer works in that situation as a weapon of attack. Prayer broke through in the heavenlies and released the intervention of angels. We can compare it to the time in Daniel 10, when Daniel prayed and the angel came from heaven with the answer.

The final comment of Scripture is in Acts 12:24:

> 24 But the word of God continued to increase and spread. (NIV)

This pictures the irresistible progress of God's Word, especially the promise that Jesus had given to Peter that he was to be an old man before he died. But it took prayer to enforce the promises of God's Word. This is what we must understand The promises of God's Word are not a substitute for our prayer, they provoke our prayer, and it takes our prayers to make the promises of God's Word effective in our spirit. It also takes our prayer to release the intervention of angels on our behalf.

The Scripture says that angels are ministering spirits, sent forth for our benefit, but they do not come, as a rule, until we pray through. By our prayer we release that intervention of angels which is God's answer. Bear in mind that prayer breaks through Satan's kingdom in the heavenlies and releases divine angelic intervention.

Chapter 16

The Weapon of Praise

The next great weapon of attack that follows logically after prayer is praise. In a sense, you could consider praise one type of prayer. In the Bible, praise is frequently related to God's awesomeness or fearfulness. Praise calls forth God's supernatural intervention and is also the appropriate response to that intervention. In Exodus 15:10-11 is found the song that Moses and Israel sang after their deliverance from Egypt and after Pharaoh's army had been destroyed by the waters of the Red Sea.

> 10 "Thou didst blow with Thy wind, the sea covered them; Thoy sank like lead in the mighty waters.
> 11 "Who is like Thee among the gods, O Lord? Who is like Thee, majestic in holiness, Awesome in praises, working wonders?" (NAS)

Note the phrase "Awesome in praises." Praise reveals and calls forth God's awesomeness, His fearfulness, especially against the enemies of God's people.

113

Psalm 22:23 declares:

> 23 You who fear the Lord, praise Him; All
> you descendants of Jacob, glorify Him, And
> stand in awe of Him, all you descendants of
> Israel.   (NAS)

Praise is the appropriate response by God's
people to His awesomeness, to His fearful acts
of war and vengeance on their behalf.

Psalm 8:2 says:

> 2 From the mouth of infants and nursing
> babes Thou hast established strength,
> Because of Thine adversaries, To make the
> enemy and the revengeful cease.   (NAS)

We see here that God has provided strength for
His people against their enemies. Two words
are used for the enemy. First,
"adversaries," in the plural. I believe this
means Satan's kingdom, in general. These are
the principalities and powers, the rulers and
authorities that are spoken of in Ephesians
6:12. The second word is "enemy," in the
singular. I believe that refers to Satan himself.

God has provided His people strength to deal
with this entire kingdom. The nature of the
strength that God has provided is more fully
revealed in Matthew 21:15-16. Jesus was in the

temple performing miracles and the little children were running to and fro crying, "Hosannah!" The religious leaders asked Jesus to silence the children.

> 15 But when the chief priests and the scribes saw the wonderful things that He had done, and the children who were crying out in the temple and saying, "Hosanna to the Son of David," they became indignant,
> 16 and said to Him, "Do You hear what these are saying?" And Jesus said to them, "Yes; have you never read, 'Out of the mouth of infants and nursing babes Thou has prepared praise for Thyself?'" (NAS)

Jesus answered them by quoting Psalm 8:2, but He changed the quotation just a little. He gave us, as it were, His own comment. The psalmist said, "Out of the mouth of infants and nursing babes Thou hast established strength." Jesus said, ". . . Thou hast prepared praise." So this reveals that the strength of God's people is praise. Praise is our great source of strength.

Notice certain other things about this revelation. First in each case it says, "Out of the mouth." The mouth is the primary channel for releasing our spiritual weapons against Satan's kingdom. Second, it speaks of

115

"infants and babes." This means those who have no natural strength of their own, who must rely on God's strength.

> 25 At that time Jesus answered and said, "I praise Thee, O Father, Lord of heaven and earth, that Thou didst hide these things from the wise and intelligent and didst reveal them to babes."
>
> (Matthew 11:25 NAS)

He was talking about His own disciples. "Babes" are not necessarily those who are just newly born in the natural, but they are those who have no natural strength of their own and must depend totally on God's strength.

The purpose of the use of praise as a weapon is to silence Satan. This lines up with Revelation 12:10. This is a vision that is yet to be fulfilled, but which tells us a great deal about Satan's activity at this time.

> 10 And I heard a loud voice in heaven, saying,
> 11 "Now the salvation, and the power, and the kingdom of our God and the authority of His Christ have come, for the accuser of our brethren has been thrown down, who accuses them before our God day and night." (NAS)

This tells us that Satan's primary activity and main weapon against us is accusations. He is accusing us continually before God, both day and night. It occurs to me that if Satan is busy day and night, we cannot afford to be busy only in the daytime. We must meet him day and night.

Satan accuses us to make us feel guilty. This is his main weapon against us.

You might say, "Well, why doesn't God silence Satan?" Simply, because God has given us the means to silence Satan and He is not going to do it for us. The means to do that is praise "out of the mouth of babes and nursing infants." It is praise that ascends through the heavenlies, reaches the throne of God, and silences Satan's accusations against us.

Revelation 16:13-14 is prophetic. I will not attempt to explain how it will be worked out in history, but I want to point out an important principle. John says:

> 13 And I saw coming out of the mouth of the dragon and out of the mouth of the beast and out of the mouth of the false prophet, three unclean spirits like frogs;
> 14 for they are spirits of demons, performing signs, which go out to the kings

of the world, to gather them together for
the war of the great day of God, the
Almighty.   (NAS)

The point I want to make here is that unclean
satanic spirits also operate through the mouth.
Praise that silences Satan comes out of the
mouths of God's people. Satanic spiritual forces
are released through the mouths of those who
are on Satan's side. Out of the mouth of the
dragon, the beast, and the false prophet came
unclean spirits. In a certain sense, this
indicates that the side which uses its mouth
most effectively will win this spiritual war. If
we do not learn to use our mouths, we cannot
win the war.

The unclean spirits are also compared to frogs.
It is interesting to note that frogs only make a
noise at night and their noise is a ceaseless,
repetitive croaking which goes on all through
the hours of darkness. I believe that is a very
vivid picture of something with which we are
familiar in contemporary civilization —
propaganda. Propaganda is often a satanic
instrument to promote false ideologies, false
political purposes, or false and evil rulers. One
of the great ways to deal with these forces is
praise that comes out of the mouth of God's
people.

Another example of the power of praise is from
Psalm 149:6-9:

> 6 May the praise of God be in their mouths
> and a double-edged sword in their hands,
> 7 to inflict vengeance on the nations and
> punishment on the peoples,
> 8 to bind their kings with fetters, their
> nobles with shackles of iron,
> 9 to carry out the sentence written against
> them. This is the glory of all his saints.
>
> (NIV)

This speaks of something that all God's saints
can do through praise. However, that praise is
accompanied by a two-edged sword, which is
God's Word. In other words, God's Word and
praise must go together. Combined with God's
Word, praise becomes an instrument of
judgment on kings and nations. The kings and
nobles referred to are Satan's angelic princes
and kings of the unseen world. To us, God's
believing people, is committed the authority to
administer on them the written sentence. In
other words, we minister on them God's
revealed judgment and this privilege is granted
to all God's saints.

In 1 Corinthians 6:2-3, Paul says to Christians:

> 2 Do you not know that the saints will
> judge the world?

3 Do you not know that we will judge angels? (NIV)

We have the authority committed to us, through God's Word and through the weapon of praise, to administer God's judgment on angels, rulers, kings, peoples and nations. That implies tremendous power and authority.

Chapter 17

The Weapon of Preaching

This weapon of attack is related even more directly and specifically to God's Word. It is solely and exclusively the preaching of God's Word. It in no way applies to the preaching of other things, such as human philosophy, political ideologies, or even elaborate theology.

We begin with the solemn charge of Paul to Timothy in 2 Timothy 4:1-4.

> 1 In the presence of God and of Christ Jesus, who will judge the living and the dead, and in view of his appearing and his kingdom, I give you this charge:
> 2 Preach the Word; be prepared in season and out of season; correct, rebuke and encourage—with great patience and careful instruction.
> 3 For the time will come when men will not put up with sound doctrine. Instead, to suit their own desires, they will gather around them a great number of teachers to say what their itching ears want to hear.

4 They will turn their ears away from the
truth and turn aside to myths.   (NIV)

I want to point out certain important things.
First, the solemnity of the charge. It is given in
the presence of God and Christ Jesus, in the
light of the fact that Christ will judge the
living and the dead and in view of His
appearing in His kingdom. It is one of the most
solemn charges ever given to a servant of God.

Second, the charge is to preach the Word. It
implies the accountability of the preacher for
what he preaches. The reference to the fact
that Jesus will judge the living and the dead
indicates the preacher will answer to the Lord
for the messages he preaches

It is a warning not to accommodate the desires
of self-pleasing rebels who do not want to hear
the truth and will look for preachers that will
preach the kind of thing they want to hear.
There is a warning that not all will receive the
truth. Nevertheless, in spite of opposition and
criticism, the charge is to preach the Word of
God.

Scripture has much to say about the
effectiveness of God's Word. In Isaiah 55:11,
God says:

11 ". . . so is my word that goes out from
my mouth: It will not return to me empty,
but will accomplish what desire and achieve
the purpose for which I sent it."   (NIV)

Again, in Jeremiah 23:29, God says:

29 "Is not my word like a fire,"
declares the Lord, "and like a hammer
that breaks a rock in pieces?"   (NIV)

Then, in Hebrews 4:12, it states:

12 The word of God is living and active.
Sharper than any double-edged sword, it
penetrates even to dividing soul and spirit,
joints and marrow; it judges the thoughts
and attitudes of the heart.   (NIV)

There is tremendous power in the preached
Word of God. Its results are guaranteed It will
not return empty. It will accomplish God's
pleasure. It is a hammer that will break in
pieces every rock that opposes the purposes of
God. It is like a sharp sword that pierces to the
innermost recesses of the human personality
and lays bare the secrets of men's hearts and
minds.

Acts 19:8-10 is an example of this power of the
preached Word of God from the ministry of
Paul in Ephesus:

8 Paul entered the synagogue and spoke boldly there for three months, arguing persuasively about the kingdom of God.

9 But some of them became obstinate; they refused to believe and publicly maligned the Way. So Paul left them. He took the disciples with him and had discussions daily in the lecture hall of Tyrannus.

10 This went on for two years, so that all the Jews and Greeks who lived in the province of Asia heard the word of the Lord. (NIV)

There are three adjectives that describe this preaching of Paul: intense, continuous, and extensive. Daily, for two years, he taught the Word of God. It was extensive in the sense that his teaching reached out to the whole of the large province of Asia. We often fail to realize that Paul spent over two years in the city of Ephesus, every day preaching the Word of God.

The results are rather like throwing a stone into a pond and then watching the ripples go out from the place where the stone fell, extending wider and wider in every direction until they reach the margin of the pond. The first result was supernatural attestation. The Scripture says that God will confirm His Word. He does not confirm human theories or philosophy, or even denominational tags. He will, however, confirm His Word. So He did for Paul. Acts 19:11-12 says:

> 11 God did extraordinary miracles through Paul. (NIV)

I love that word "extraordinary miracles." Do you know what that implies? That some miracles were ordinary but the ones that happened here in Ephesus were extraordinary.

I have asked myself this question: "In how many of our churches today do we have even ordinary miracles, let alone extraordinary miracles?" These extraordinary miracles are then described:

> 12 Handkerchiefs and aprons that had touched him were taken to the sick, and their illnesses were cured and the evil spirits left them. (NIV)

I can testify from personal experience that I have seen miracles like that happen in my time. This practice is not out of date. The key factor is preaching the Word of God.

The first result of Paul's preaching in Ephesus was supernatural attestation to his message by miracles. The second result is evil spirits being driven out into the open. Acts 19:13-16 says:

13 Some Jews who went around driving out evil spirits tried to invoke the name of the Lord Jesus over those who were demon-possessed. They would say, "In the name of Jesus whom Paul preaches, I command you to come out."

14 Seven sons of Sceva, a Jewish chief priest, were doing this.

15 The evil spirit answered them, "Jesus I know and Paul I know about, but who are you?"

16 Then the man who had the evil spirit jumped on them and overpowered them all. He gave them such a beating that they ran out of the house naked and bleeding.(NIV)

One of the important things in the ministry is to bring Satan's secret agents out into the open. Demons, or evil spirits, are Satan's secret agents. It represents a great stage of progress in the ministry of God's Word when these evil spirits are brought right out into the open. That is what happened here I am impressed by what the evil spirit said: "Jesus I acknowledge, Paul I know about." To me, that is a kind of back-handed compliment when the representatives of Satan can say about a preacher, "I know about him; he is achieving something."

The third result of Paul's preaching was the occult domination over an entire city was broken, as described in Acts 19:17-19:

17 When this [the incident of the man with the evil spirit] became known to the Jews and Greeks living in Ephesus, they were all seized with fear, and the name of the Lord Jesus was held in high honor.

18 Many of those who believed now came and openly confessed their evil deeds.

19 A number who had practiced sorcery brought their scrolls together and burned them publicly. When they calculated the value of the scrolls, the total came to fifty thousand drachmas. (NIV)

You see, a lot of people were believers but they had been dabbling in the occult, a situation that is similar in the church today. They had one foot in God's kingdom, one foot in Satan's camp. But when they saw this fearful demonstration of the reality of Satan's power, they decided to commit themselves totally to God and turn their back on Satan. As evidence of this, they brought the books or the scrolls, which contained the occult knowledge, magic, and sorcery. All these books were publicly burned in the city of Ephesus.

The value of the books were fifty thousand drachmas. A drachma, at that time, was about a day's wages for a working man. If you estimate a day's wages in the United States at about $30, fifty thousand drachmas corresponds to $1,500,000. That is a large sum of money. The same thing needs to happen in almost every major city of the United States today.

Let us look at the Scripture's explanation of all this in Acts 19:20:

> 20 In this way the word of the Lord spread widely and grew in power. (NIV)

The power behind all this was the Word of the Lord. Paul's ministry of the Word for over two years produced dramatic, powerful results. Satan's kingdom in that area was rocked to its foundations, his fortresses were overthrown.

Acts 20:20 and following is Paul's own account of his ministry in Ephesus:

> 20 You know that I have not hesitated to preach anything that would be helpful to you. . .
> 26 Therefore, I declare to you today that I am innocent of the blood of all men.
> 27 For I have not hesitated to proclaim to you the whole will of God. (NIV)

Paul summed up his ministry as one having no reservation and no compromise. That is the kind of preaching of the Word of God that accomplishes similar effects. We need that type of preaching today.

Chapter 18

The Weapon of Testimony

We need to begin by distinguishing between testimony and preaching. Preaching is presenting the truths of God's Word directly, but testimony is "witnessing" or "being a witness." Testimony is speaking from personal experience about incidents that relate to the Word of God and confirm the truth of God's Word. For instance, if we are preaching a message on healing, we preach the principles on which God heals and we offer His promises of healing. But if we are testifying about healing, we speak about an incident in which we experienced God healing us. So testimony and preaching are both related to the Word of God but they approach it from different angles.

Testimony is basic to Jesus' strategy of reaching the whole world with the gospel. He unveiled this strategy in His closing words on earth as He stood on the Mount of Olives with

His disciples, about to leave them, as found in Acts 1:8:

> 8 "But you will receive power when the Holy Spirit comes on you; and you will be my witnesses in Jerusalem, and in all Judea and Samaria, and to the end of the earth." (NIV)

We notice, first, that to be effective witnesses for Jesus, we need supernatural power. Our testimony is supernatural. It needs to be backed and enforced by supernatural power, the power of the Holy Spirit. Jesus did not permit His disciples to go out and begin testifying until they had been endued with that power on the Day of Pentecost.

Second, Jesus did not say, "You will witness," which is what a lot of religious people say today. He said, "You will be witnesses. . ." In other words, it is not just the words we speak or the tracts that we hand out, but our total life is to be a witness to Jesus and the truth of the gospel.

Third, Jesus envisaged an ever-extending circle. He said start where you are in Jerusalem. Go and tell people. Let them believe and let them be filled with the Holy Spirit. Then let them go and tell other people. In turn, let them believe, be filled with the Holy Spirit, and go and tell others. He said it will start in Jerusalem, move out to Judea, then to Samaria, and will not cease until it reaches the outermost part of the earth.

Those were the last words Jesus spoke on earth. His mind and His heart were in the uttermost part of the earth. He would never be satisfied until that had been reached. His basic strategy for reaching it was for all God's people to become witnesses, witnessing to and winning others. Those, in turn, were to witness and win until, like the expanding ripples from stones cast into a pond, they reached the uttermost part of the earth.

Looking back on history, when God's people applied this strategy, it worked. Within three hundred years, it had conquered the Roman Empire. I believe that great basic spiritual force that overthrew the pagan Roman Empire was the testimony of thousands and thousands of Christian believers from different backgrounds, races, social levels, and religious persuasions. They all said, "Jesus changed my life!" The impact of this ultimately broke down that stern, strong, cruel empire of Rome.

The Bible indicates that the same weapon will ultimately cast down even Satan's kingdom in the heavenlies. This can be seen in prophetic preview in Revelation 12:7-11. These verses describe a great conflict which will span both heaven and earth at the close of this age between angels and men.

> 7 And there was war in heaven. [I believe that is still in the future.] Michael and his angels fought against the dragon, and the dragon and his angels fought back
> 8 But he was not strong enough, and they lost their place in heaven.
> 9 The great dragon was hurled down—that ancient serpent called the devil or Satan, who leads the whole world astray. He was hurled to the earth, and his angels with him.
> 10 Then I heard a loud voice in heaven say: "Now have come the salvation and the power and the kingdom of our God, and the authority of his Christ. For the accuser of our brothers, who accuses them before our God day and night, has been hurled down." (NIV)

The "accuser of the brothers" is Satan. This describes how he has been hurled down from his kingdom in the heavenlies. Then it describes how the believers overcame Satan. Notice it is a direct, person-to-person conflict.

> 11 "They [the believers] overcame him [Satan] by the blood of the Lamb and by the word of their testimony they did not love

132

their lives so much as to shrink from
death." (NIV)

Their main weapon is in that word
"testimony." It is their testimony that will
ultimately shake down the whole kingdom of
Satan. I believe their testimony centers in two
things: the Word of God and the blood of Jesus.
Their testimony released the power that is in
the Word and the blood.

We can apply this in a simple, practical way to
ourselves. **We overcome Satan when we
testify personally to what the Word of God
says the blood of Jesus does for us.** You
can see the importance of bearing personal
testimony to the Word and to the blood.

There are various ways we can do that. One
appointed way is the Lord's Supper or the
Eucharist. Sometimes we do not see it in this
light, but this is a continuing testimony of our
faith in the Word and the blood. Speaking
about the Lord's Supper, Paul said in 1
Corinthians 11:26:

> 26 For whenever you eat this bread and
> drink this cup, you proclaim the Lord's
> death until he comes. (NIV)

We know the cup represents the blood of the
Lord, so in taking the Lord's Supper, we are

133

continually testifying, proclaiming the death and resurrection of Jesus Christ.

In order to testify effectively to what the Word of God says about the blood of Jesus, we must be familiar with what the Word of God actually tells us about the blood of Jesus. There are five extremely important provisions revealed in God's Word that come to us through the blood of Jesus.

First, we find in Ephesians 1:7:

> 7 In him [Christ] we have redemption through his blood, the forgiveness of sins, in accordance with the riches of God's grace. . . .
> (NIV)

That tells us two things that are provided for us through the blood of Jesus. First is redemption (we are redeemed). Second is forgiveness (we are forgiven), as shown in 1 John 1:7:

> 7 . . . but if we walk in the light as He himself is in the light, we have fellowship with one another, and the blood of Jesus His Son cleanses us from all sin.   (NAS)

Third, the blood cleanses us continually. Through the blood, we have available to us continual spiritual cleansing. Romans 5:9 states:

> 9 Much more then, having now been justified by His blood, we shall be saved from the wrath of God through Him.
>
> (NAS)

Fourth, we are justified. That means we are made righteous. The best description ever heard of "justified" is: Justified, just-as-if-I'd never sinned, because I have been made righteous with a righteousness that knows no sin, which is the righteousness of Christ.

Hebrews 13:12 declares:

> 12 Therefore Jesus also, that He might sanctify the people through His own blood, suffered outside the gate.　　(NAS)

Fifth, the Bible tells us that we can be sanctified through the blood of Jesus. "To sanctify" means to make holy, or to set apart to God.

These are the five great provisions of the blood of Jesus revealed by the Word of God:

First, we are redeemed;

Second, we are forgiven;

Third, we are cleansed;

Fourth, we are justified (made righteous);

Fifth, we are sanctified (made holy).

These provisions only become fully effective in our lives when we testify to them personally. We must be bold enough to state our convictions. We must say it like this:

> Through the blood of Jesus, I am redeemed out of the hand of Satan. Through the blood of Jesus, all my sins are forgiven. The blood of Jesus cleanses me from all sins. Through the blood of Jesus, I am justified, made righteous, just-as-if-I'd never sinned. Through the blood of Jesus, I am sanctified, made holy, set apart to God. I am no longer in Satan's territory.

Meditate on those five provisions of the blood of Jesus: redemption, forgiveness, cleansing, justification, sanctification. Then grasp the fact that they become effectually yours when you testify to them personally. By testifying to them personally, we overcome Satan "by the blood of the Lamb and by the word of our testimony."

To be effective in spiritual warfare, we must continually take the offensive with the weapons

God has provided for us. It is not sufficient to merely defend ourselves and wait for the Lord to deliver us. We are an army of conquerors, and the nations of the world are ripe for a people who will conquer them with the Gospel of the Kingdom.